W0018939

Ponies and
Horses

FIRST EDITION
Series Editor Deborah Lock; **US Editor** John Searcy;
Project Art Editor Mary Sandberg; **Production Editor** Siu Yin Chan; **Production** Claire Pearson;
Jacket Designer Mary Sandberg; **Reading Consultant** Linda Gambrell, PhD

THIS EDITION
Editorial Management by Oriel Square
Produced for DK by WonderLab Group LLC
Jennifer Emmett, Erica Green, Kate Hale, *Founders*

Editors Grace Hill Smith, Libby Romero, Michaela Weglinski;
Photography Editors Kelley Miller, Annette Kiesow, Nicole DiMella;
Managing Editor Rachel Houghton; **Designers** Project Design Company;
Researcher Michelle Harris; **Copy Editor** Lori Merritt; **Indexer** Connie Binder;
Proofreader Larry Shea; **Reading Specialist** Dr. Jennifer Albro; **Curriculum Specialist** Elaine Larson

Published in the United States by DK Publishing
1745 Broadway, 20th Floor, New York, NY 10019

Copyright © 2023 Dorling Kindersley Limited
DK, a Division of Penguin Random House LLC
24 25 26 27 28 10 9 8 7 6 5 4 3 2 1
001–341822–Mar/2024

All rights reserved.
Without limiting the rights under the copyright reserved
above, no part of this publication may be reproduced, stored
in or introduced into a retrieval system, or transmitted, in any
form, or by any means (electronic, mechanical, photocopying,
recording, or otherwise), without the prior written permission
of the copyright owner.
Published in Great Britain by Dorling Kindersley Limited

A catalog record for this book
is available from the Library of Congress.
ISBN: 978-0-5938-4252-2

DK books are available at special discounts when purchased
in bulk for sales promotions, premiums, fundraising, or
educational use. For details, contact: DK Publishing Special Markets,
1745 Broadway, 20th Floor, New York, NY 10019
SpecialSales@dk.com

Printed and bound in China

The publisher would like to thank the following for their kind permission to reproduce their images:
a=above; c=center; b=below; l=left; r=right; t=top; b/g=background

Alamy: Peter Llewellyn 17; **Corbis:** Walter Bieri / EPA 22; **Dreamstime.com:** Warangkana Charuyodhin 4-5,
Elena Titarenco 12, 13; **DK Images:** Miss. H Houlden ac, Stephen Oliver 2t, 8c; **FLPA:** Gerard Lacz 18–19; **Getty Images:**
Gallo Images / Travel Ink 6-7b; **Getty Images / iStock:** NiKita Filippov 20-21; **Masterfile:** R. Ian Lloyd 26-27; **Shutterstock:**
Picture Partners 9, Kondrashov MIkhail Evgenevich 16, Dennis Donohue 24-25; **SuperStock:** Age Fotostock 28-29

Cover images: *Front:* **123RF.com:** Olga Itina b; **Shutterstock:** Macrovector tr, br, Vector_Up;
Back: **Shutterstock:** Macrovector tl, cra, bl

All other images © Dorling Kindersley Limited

www.dk.com

MIX
Paper | Supporting
responsible forestry
FSC™ C018179

This book was made with Forest
Stewardship Council™ certified
paper - one small step in DK's
commitment to a sustainable future.
**For more information go to
www.dk.com/our-green-pledge**

Ponies and Horses

Fiona Lock

Contents

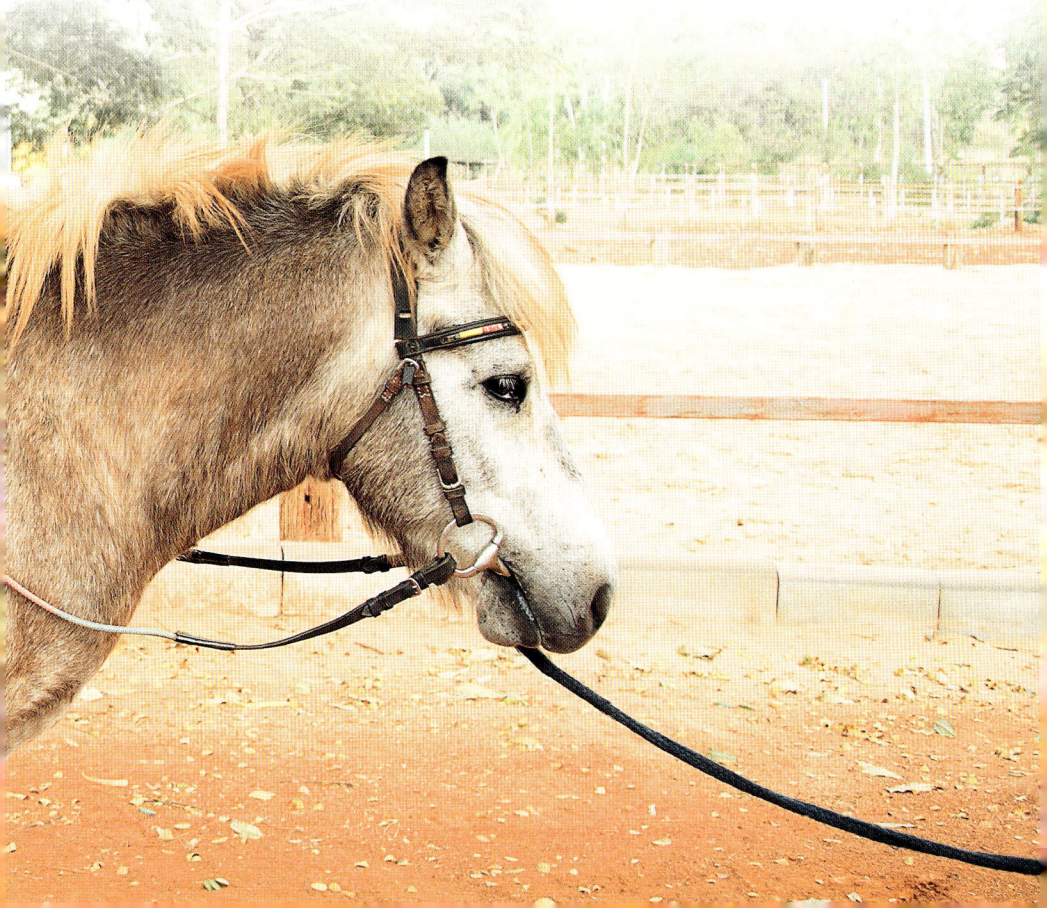

Welcome to
the stable yard.
This is where the horses
eat and drink.

hay

Pony

The pony has to be brushed and washed.

brush

grooming kit

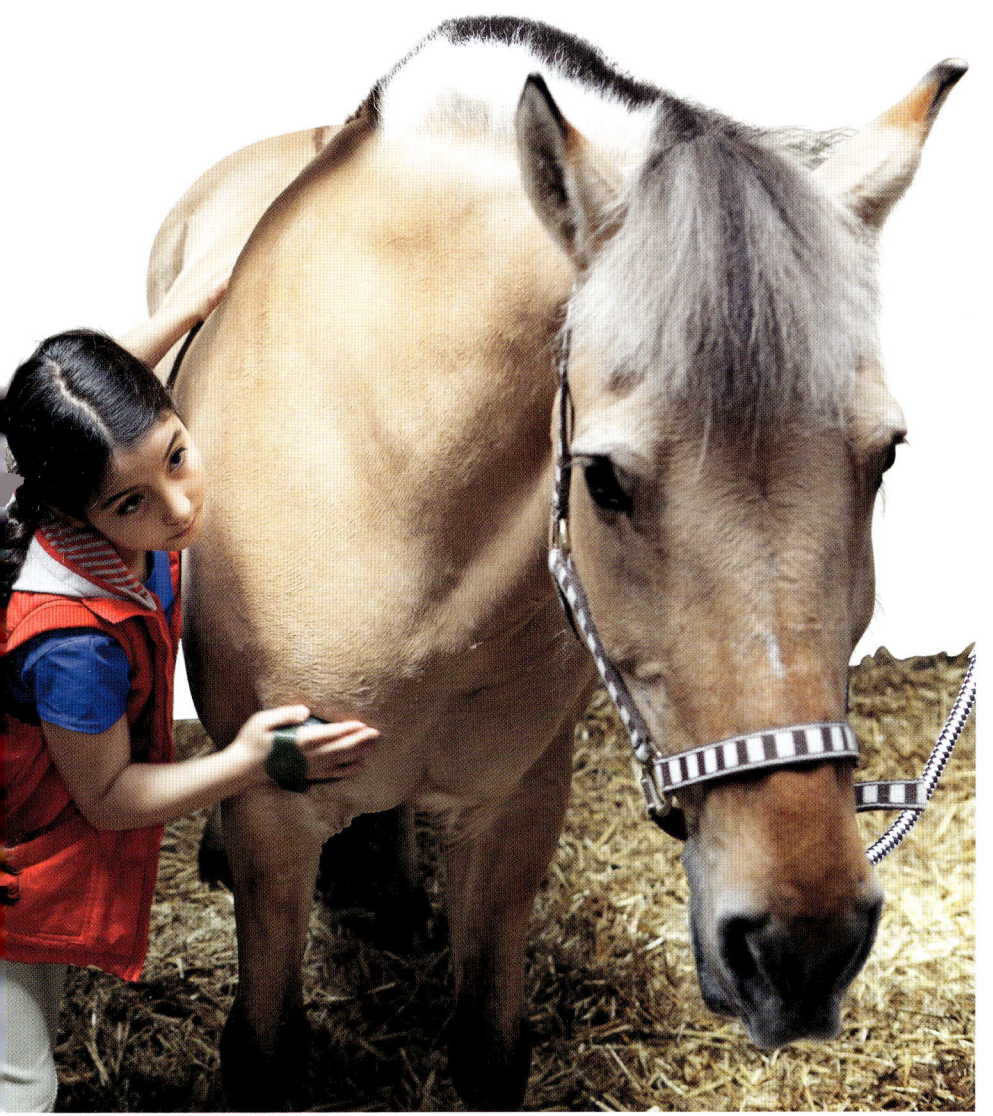

Brown Horse

The brown horse has horseshoes fitted to its hooves.

horseshoe

Palomino Pony

The rider puts a saddle on the palomino pony.

palomino pony
[pal-uh-MEE-no]

saddle

Chestnut Horses

The chestnut horses go for a walk wearing bridles. The riders wear riding hats.

riding hat

bridle

Black Horse

The black horse at the horse show performs tricks for people.

stirrup

Gray Pony

The rider tells
the gray pony to trot
and then to canter.

rider

Bay Horse

The reddish-brown bay horse jumps over the fence.

fence

Dancing Horses

The dancing horses jump and leap.

hooves

Racehorses

The racehorses race around the track.

Who will win?

jockey

track

Ranch Horses

Ranchers ride ranch horses to round up the cattle.

rancher

cattle

Wild Horses

The wild horses gallop across a river.

Glossary

brush
a tool for brushing the hair of a horse

fence
a row of bars for a horse to jump over

hooves
the feet of a horse

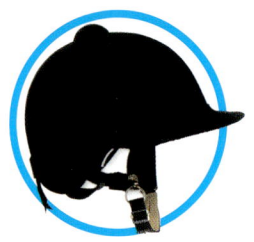

riding hat
a hard hat that a rider wears

saddle
a seat for a rider that is tied onto a horse's back

Index

Quiz

Answer the questions to see what you have learned. Check your answers with an adult.

1. What is fitted to a horse's hooves?

2. What do a rider and horse do at a horse show?

3. What is the rider of a racehorse called?

4. What do ranchers and ranch horses do?

5. What would you like to do if you had your own horse? How would you take care of your horse?

1. Horseshoes 2. Perform tricks for people 3. A jockey
4. Round up cattle 5. Answers will vary

Nighttime Animals

FIRST EDITION
Series Editor Deborah Lock; **US Senior** Editor Shannon Beatty; **Art Director** Martin Wilson;
Designer Yamini Panwar; **Picture Researcher** Surya Sarangi;
Senior Producer, Pre-Production Ben Marcus; **Jacket Designer** Martin Wilson;
Reading Consultant Linda Gambrell, PhD

THIS EDITION
Editorial Management by Oriel Square
Produced for DK by WonderLab Group LLC
Jennifer Emmett, Erica Green, Kate Hale, *Founders*

Editors Grace Hill Smith, Libby Romero, Maya Myers, Michaela Weglinski;
Photography Editors Kelley Miller, Annette Kiesow, Nicole DiMella;
Managing Editor Rachel Houghton; **Designers** Project Design Company;
Researcher Michelle Harris; **Copy Editor** Lori Merritt; **Indexer** Connie Binder;
Proofreader Larry Shea; **Reading Specialist** Dr. Jennifer Albro; **Curriculum Specialist** Elaine Larson

Published in the United States by DK Publishing
1745 Broadway, 20th Floor, New York, NY 10019

Copyright © 2023 Dorling Kindersley Limited
DK, a Division of Penguin Random House LLC
24 25 26 27 28 10 9 8 7 6 5 4 3 2 1
001–341822–Mar/2024

All rights reserved.
Without limiting the rights under the copyright reserved above, no part of this publication may be reproduced, stored in or
introduced into a retrieval system, or transmitted, in any form, or by any means (electronic, mechanical, photocopying,
recording, or otherwise), without the prior written permission of the copyright owner.
Published in Great Britain by Dorling Kindersley Limited

A catalog record for this book
is available from the Library of Congress.
ISBN: 978-0-5938-4252-2

DK books are available at special discounts when purchased in bulk for sales promotions, premiums,
fundraising, or educational use. For details, contact: DK Publishing Special Markets,
1745 Broadway, 20th Floor, New York, NY 10019
SpecialSales@dk.com

Printed and bound in China

The publisher would like to thank the following for their kind permission to reproduce their images:
a=above; c=center; b=below; l=left; r=right; t=top; b/g=background

Dreamstime.com: Hotshotsworldwide 22c, Ondej Prosick 4-5, Tifonimages 28-29

Cover images: *Front:* **Dreamstime.com:** Krissikunterbunt b; **Shutterstock.com:** johnpluto tl, Propex;
Back: **Dreamstime.com:** Pavel Naumov cra

All other images © Dorling Kindersley
For more information see: www.dkimages.com

www.dk.com

MIX
Paper | Supporting
responsible forestry
FSC™ C018179

This book was made with Forest
Stewardship Council™ certified
paper - one small step in DK's
commitment to a sustainable future.
For more information go to
www.dk.com/our-green-pledge

Level

1

Nighttime Animals

Contents

Night Falls

The sun sets.
The nighttime animals
wake up.
It's time to eat.

Coyotes

Coyotes run and hunt.
They call to each other.

Owls

Owls look and listen. Then they swoop in to catch an animal.

wing

talon

Moths

Moths fly around in the moonlight.

Scorpions

Scorpions lift their stingers. They are ready to attack.

stinger

claw

Boa Constrictors

A boa constrictor slithers along a branch.

It searches
for food.

Lorises

Lorises see in the dark with wide-open eyes.

eye

finger

Raccoons

Raccoons scamper over logs.

They will eat any food they can find.

fur

Possums

Possums scurry around with their babies, called joeys.

joey

Bats

Bats fly around at night. They squeak through their noses.

nose

Leopards

A leopard hunts alone. Its glowing eye scan see very well in the dark.

eye

ear

The Day Begins

The sun rises.
The nighttime
animals sleep.
It's been a
busy night.

Glossary

fur
the hair that grows
on the bodies of
many mammals

joey
young possum

stinger
stinging part
of an insect

talon
sharp claw of a bird

wing
arm of a bird covered
with feathers

Index

Quiz

Answer the questions to see what you have learned. Check your answers with an adult.

1. Which animal uses a stinger to attack?

2. Which animal has wide-open eyes to see in the dark?

3. Which animal eats any food it can find?

4. Which animal squeaks through its nose?

5. Which animal has glowing eyes?

1. Scorpion 2. Loris 3. Raccoon 4. Bat 5. Leopard

Explore the
Coral Reef

FIRST EDITION

Series Editor Deborah Lock; **US Senior Editor** Shannon Beatty; **Editor** Arpita Nath;
Design Assistant Sadie Thomas; **Art Editor** Dheeraj Arora; **Senior Art Editor** Tory Gordon-Harris;
Producer Sara Hu; **Pre-Production Producer** Nadine King; **Jacket Designer** Natalie Godwin;
Managing Editor Soma Chowdhury; **Managing Art Editor** Ahlawat Gunjan;
Art Directors Rachel Foster and Martin Wilson; **Reading Consultant** Linda Gambrell, PhD

THIS EDITION

Editorial Management by Oriel Square
Produced for DK by WonderLab Group LLC
Jennifer Emmett, Erica Green, Kate Hale, *Founders*

Editors Grace Hill Smith, Libby Romero, Michaela Weglinski;
Photography Editors Kelley Miller, Annette Kiesow, Nicole DiMella;
Managing Editor Rachel Houghton; **Designers** Project Design Company; **Researcher** Michelle Harris;
Copy Editor Lori Merritt; **Indexer** Connie Binder; **Proofreader** Larry Shea;
Reading Specialist Dr. Jennifer Albro; **Curriculum Specialist** Elaine Larson

Published in the United States by DK Publishing
1745 Broadway, 20th Floor, New York, NY 10019

Copyright © 2023 Dorling Kindersley Limited
DK, a Division of Penguin Random House LLC
24 25 26 27 28 10 9 8 7 6 5 4 3 2 1
001–341822–Mar/2024

All rights reserved.
Without limiting the rights under the copyright reserved
above, no part of this publication may be reproduced, stored
in or introduced into a retrieval system, or transmitted, in any
form, or by any means (electronic, mechanical, photocopying,
recording, or otherwise), without the prior written permission
of the copyright owner.
Published in Great Britain by Dorling Kindersley Limited

A catalog record for this book
is available from the Library of Congress.
ISBN: 978-0-5938-4252-2

DK books are available at special discounts when purchased
in bulk for sales promotions, premiums, fundraising, or
educational use. For details, contact: DK Publishing Special Markets,
1745 Broadway, 20th Floor, New York, NY 10019
SpecialSales@dk.com

Printed and bound in China

The publisher would like to thank the following for their kind permission to reproduce their images:
a=above; c=center; b=below; l=left; r=right; t=top; b/g=background

Dorling Kindersley: Tina Gong 10c; **Dreamstime.com:** Luca Gialdini 20, Ingrid Prats / Titania1980 3;
Getty Images / iStock: strmko 4-5; **Shutterstock.com:** Sergius Bleicher 24-25, Rich Carey 10-11, Diman_Diver 21,
Rostislav Stefanek 26-27, Stock for you 19cra

Cover images: *Front:* **Dreamstime.com:** John Anderson b, Artisticco Llc; *Back:* **Dreamstime.com:** Andrii Symonenko bl

All other images © Dorling Kindersley

www.dk.com

MIX
Paper | Supporting
responsible forestry
FSC™ C018179

This book was made with Forest
Stewardship Council™ certified
paper - one small step in DK's
commitment to a sustainable future.
**For more information go to
www.dk.com/our-green-pledge**

Level

1

Explore the
coral Reef

Deborah Lock

Contents

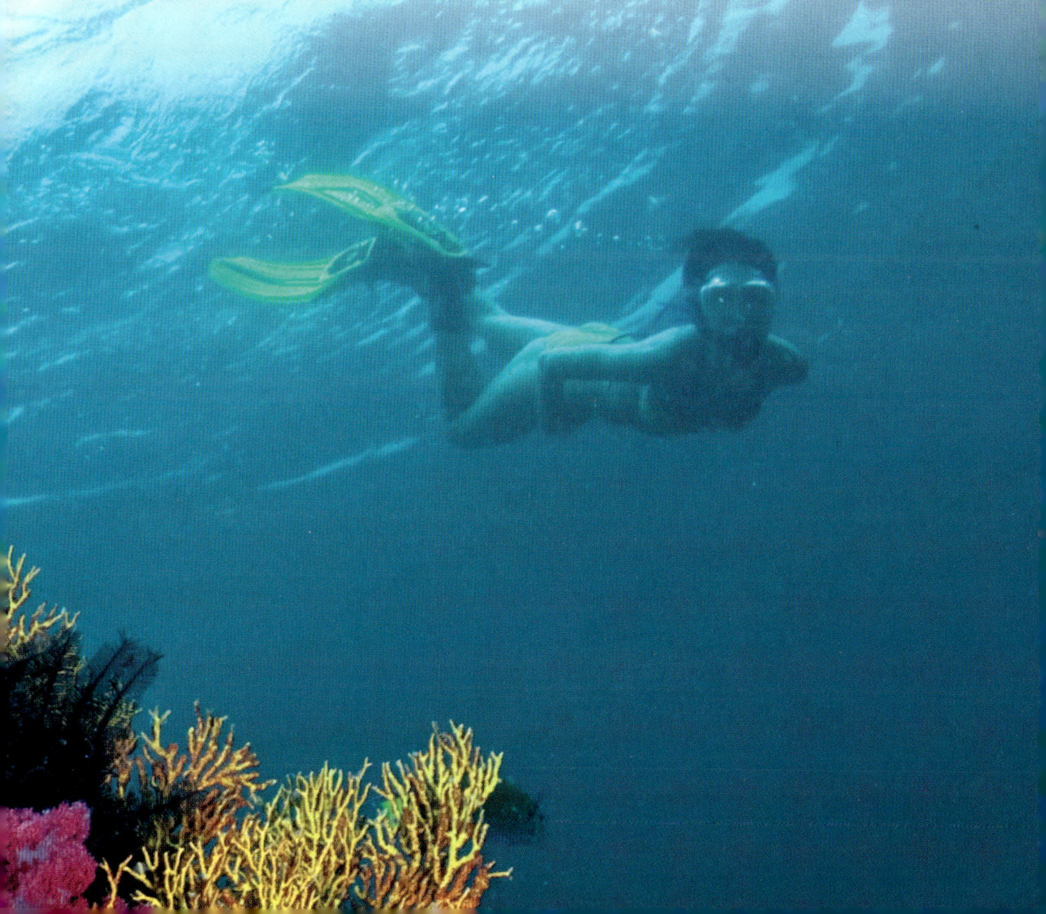

Coral

Here is a coral reef.

What animals do you see?

coral

fish

Sea Turtles

The sea turtles play in the ocean.

shell

flipper

Seahorses

The seahorses sway to and fro.

tail

snout

fin

arm

Sea Stars

Sea stars crawl
on the ocean floor.

Jellyfish

Jellyfish float
up and down
in the ocean.

tentacles

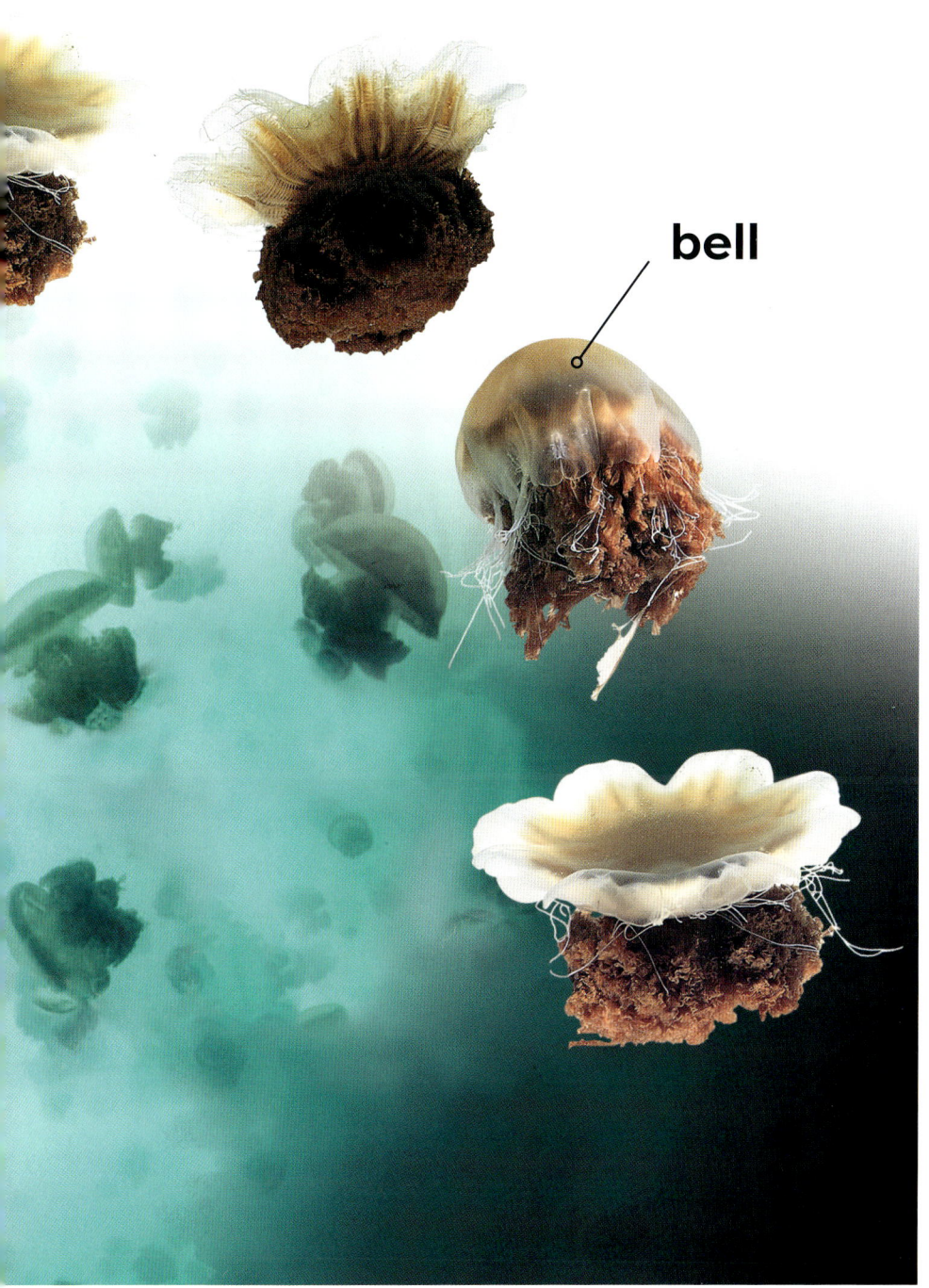

bell

tail

Sharks

Here comes a shark.
It looks for food.

fin

mouth

Octopuses

An octopus shoots off to hide.

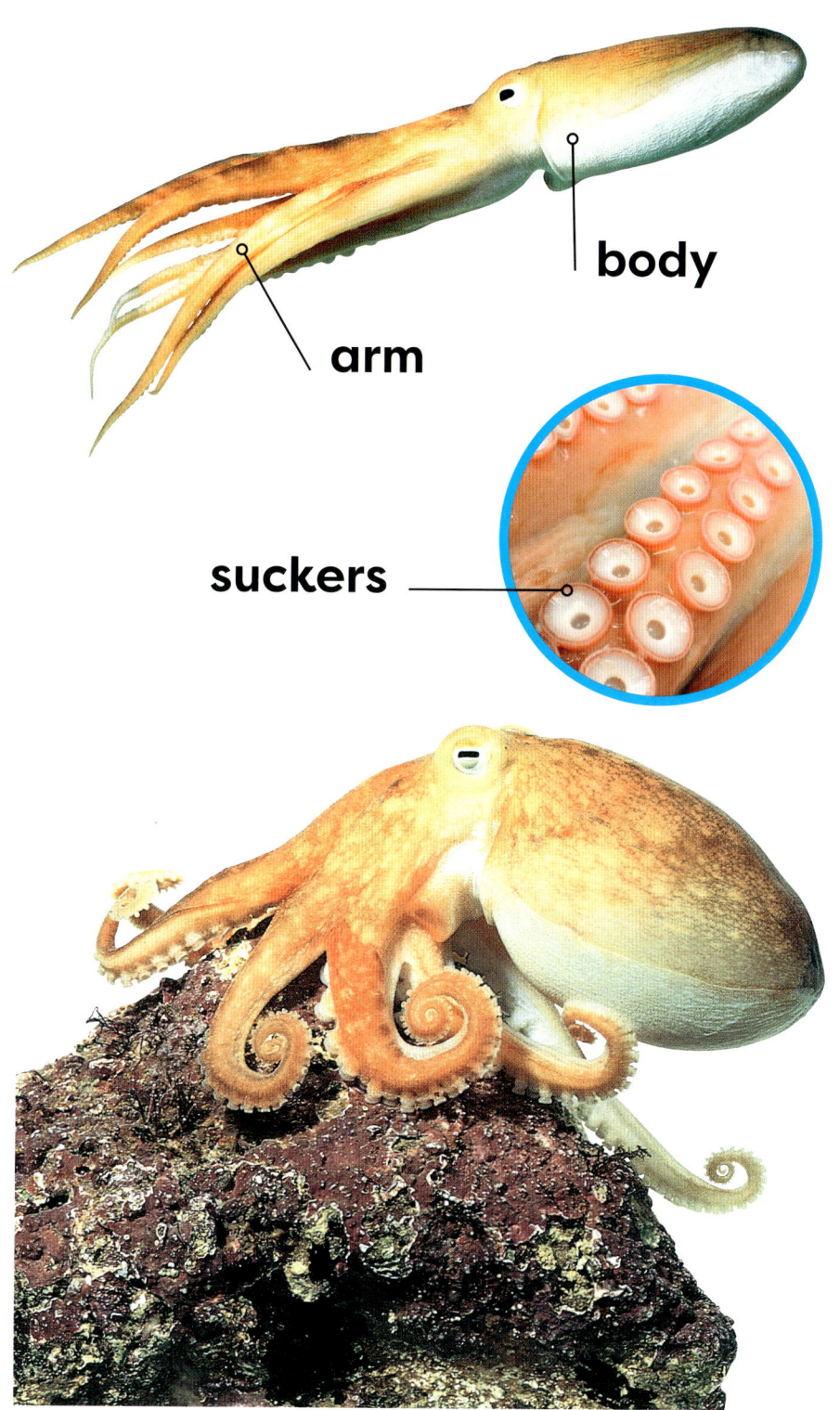

body

arm

suckers

Crabs

Crabs hide in
the coral and
inside big shells.

shell

leg

claw

21

Rays

A ray hides on
the ocean floor.

tail

hiding

eye

fin

Dolphins

A dolphin swims away. It moves its tail up and down.

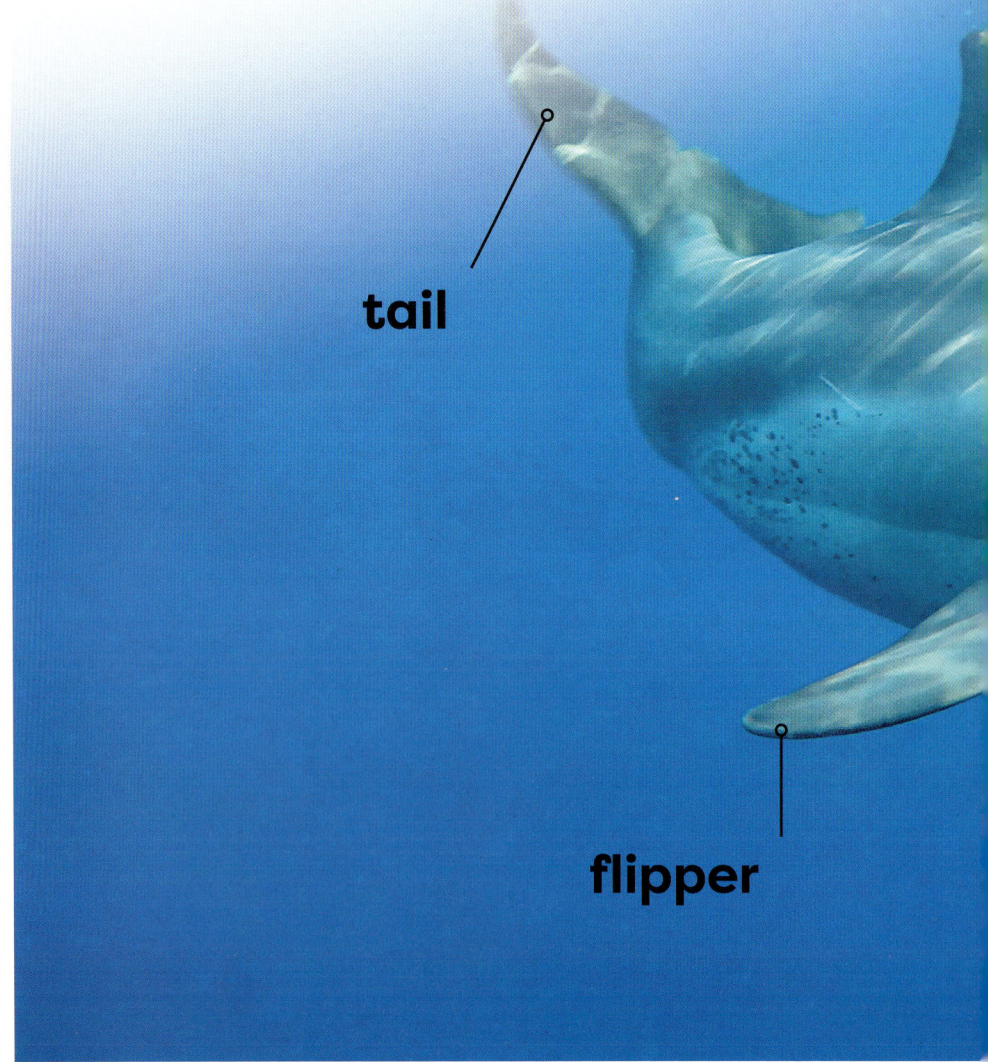

tail

flipper

mouth

Eels

An eel looks out for the shark.

eye

tail

fin

The shark swims away.

gills

nose

Glossary

eel
a snake-like fish

octopus
a sea animal with eight long arms

ray
a flat fish with large wing-like fins

sea star
a sea animal with five arms shaped like a star

sea turtle
a marine reptile with a domed shell

Index

Quiz

Answer the questions to see what you have learned. Check your answers with an adult.

Which sea animal am I?

1. I have flippers and a hard shell.

2. I have a bell and tentacles.

3. I have long arms covered in suckers.

4. I hide in coral and inside big shells.

5. I am a fish with a long tail and small fins.

1. A sea turtle 2. A jellyfish 3. An octopus
4. A crab 5. An eel

JUNGLE ANIMALS

FIRST EDITION
Project Editor Deborah Murrell; **Art Editor** Catherine Goldsmith; **US Editor** Regina Kahney;
Pre-Production Producer Nadine King; **Producer** Sara Hu; **Picture Researcher** Frances Vargo;
Picture Librarian Sally Hamilton; **Jacket Designer** Natalie Godwin;
Publishing Manager Bridget Giles; **Reading Consultant** Linda Gambrell PhD

THIS EDITION
Editorial Management by Oriel Square
Produced for DK by WonderLab Group LLC
Jennifer Emmett, Erica Green, Kate Hale, *Founders*

Editors Grace Hill Smith, Libby Romero, Michaela Weglinski;
Photography Editors Kelley Miller, Annette Kiesow, Nicole DiMella;
Managing Editor Rachel Houghton; **Designers** Project Design Company; **Researcher** Michelle Harris;
Copy Editor Lori Merritt; **Indexer** Connie Binder; **Proofreader** Larry Shea;
Reading Specialist Dr. Jennifer Albro; **Curriculum Specialist** Elaine Larson

Published in the United States by DK Publishing
1745 Broadway, 20th Floor, New York, NY 10019

Copyright © 2023 Dorling Kindersley Limited
DK, a Division of Penguin Random House LLC
24 25 26 27 28 10 9 8 7 6 5 4 3 2 1
001–341822–Mar/2024

All rights reserved.

Without limiting the rights under the copyright reserved above, no part of this publication may be reproduced, stored in or
introduced into a retrieval system, or transmitted, in any form, or by any means (electronic, mechanical, photocopying,
recording, or otherwise), without the prior written permission of the copyright owner.
Published in Great Britain by Dorling Kindersley Limited

A catalog record for this book
is available from the Library of Congress.
ISBN: 978-0-5938-4252-2

DK books are available at special discounts when purchased in bulk for sales promotions, premiums,
fundraising, or educational use. For details, contact: DK Publishing Special Markets,
1745 Broadway, 20th Floor, New York, NY 10019
SpecialSales@dk.com

Printed and bound in China

The publisher would like to thank the following for their kind permission to reproduce their images:
a=above; c=center; b=below; l=left; r=right; t=top; b/g=background

Alamy Stock Photo: Glyn Thomas 16cb; **Dreamstime.com:** Aechevaphoto 4-5, Harry Collins 14-15,
Dirk Ercken 25tr, 25ca, Andrey Gudkov 6-7, Pljvv 18-19, Roman Samokhin 3cb; **Getty Images:** Corbis / Fuse 27ca;
Getty Images / iStock: Artush 8-9; naturepl.com: Eric Baccega 18ca, Anup Shah 12-13;
Shutterstock.com: Dirk Ercken 24-25, 30bl, Lucas.Barros 11tl, Michail_Vorobyev 16-17

Cover images: *Front:* **Shutterstock.com:** ActiveLines, Stepan Kapl c, Nikolai Zaburdaev b;
Back: **Shutterstock.com:** Macrovector clb

All other images © Dorling Kindersley
For more information see: www.dkimages.com

www.dk.com

MIX
Paper | Supporting
responsible forestry
FSC™ C018179

This book was made with Forest
Stewardship Council™ certified
paper - one small step in DK's
commitment to a sustainable future.
**For more information go to
www.dk.com/our-green-pledge**

Level
1

JUNGLE ANIMALS

Camilla Gersh

Contents

Enter the jungle,
if you dare!
Look up! Look down!
Look out!

Parrots

A parrot flies over the jungle. Its feathers flash red, yellow, and blue.

feathers

Toucans

A toucan picks
a berry with
its large, yellow beak.

beak

Orangutans

Orangutans swing from tree to tree.
They move very quickly.

Sloths

Sloths live in trees. They move very, very slowly.

Sun Bears

Sun bears climb
the trees.
Their long claws
grip the branches.

claws

Gorillas

Gorillas live
with their families.

nest

They make nests
to sleep in at night.

Giant Anteaters

An anteater sniffs
an ants' nest
with its long snout.

snout

ants' nest

Tarantulas

A tarantula feels the ground shake with its hairy legs.

hairy leg

A tasty meal is moving nearby!

Poison Dart Frogs

A poison dart frog protects itself with its poison skin.

Tigers

A tiger hides
in the grass.
It watches and waits,
ready to leap.

Jaguars

A jaguar rests.
Shh!
Quiet in the jungle,
please!

Glossary

beak
a hard, pointed bird's mouth

claws
sharp nails used to hold, climb, and grab

feathers
a soft covering on a bird's body

snout
a long, pointed nose and mouth used to smell and eat

skin
the outer layer of an animal, beneath fur and feathers

Index

Quiz

Answer the questions to see what you have learned. Check your answers with an adult.

1. Which jungle animal has red, yellow, and blue feathers?

2. Which jungle animal moves very, very slowly?

3. What does a giant anteater do with its long snout?

4. Which jungle animal has poison skin?

5. Name three other jungle animals. What do they do in the jungle?

1. A parrot 2. A sloth 3. It sniffs an ants' nest
4. A poison dart frog 5. Answers will vary

FROZEN
Worlds

DK | Penguin Random House

FIRST EDITION

Project Editor Allison Singer; **Assistant Editor** Prerna Grewal; **US Senior** Editor Shannon Beatty; **Art Editors** Emma Hobson, Mohd Zishan; **Jacket Editor** Francesca Young; **Jacket Designers** Amy Keast, Dheeraj Arora; **DTP Designer** Dheeraj Singh; **Picture Researcher** Sakshi Saluja; **Producer, Pre-Production** Nadine King; **Producer** Niamh Tierney; **Managing Editors** Laura Gilbert, Monica Saigal; **Managing Art Editors** Diane Peyton Jones, Neha Ahuja Chowdhry; **Art Director** Martin Wilson; **Publisher** Sarah Larter; **Publishing Director** Sophie Mitchell; **Reading Consultant** Linda Gambrell PhD

THIS EDITION

Editorial Management by Oriel Square
Produced for DK by WonderLab Group LLC
Jennifer Emmett, Erica Green, Kate Hale, *Founders*

Editors Grace Hill Smith, Libby Romero, Michaela Weglinski; **Photography Editors** Kelley Miller, Annette Kiesow, Nicole DiMella; **Managing Editor** Rachel Houghton; **Designers** Project Design Company; **Researcher** Michelle Harris; **Copy Editor** Lori Merritt; **Indexer** Connie Binder; **Proofreader** Larry Shea; **Reading Specialist** Dr. Jennifer Albro; **Curriculum Specialist** Elaine Larson

Published in the United States by DK Publishing
1745 Broadway, 20th Floor, New York, NY 10019

Copyright © 2023 Dorling Kindersley Limited
DK, a Division of Penguin Random House LLC
24 25 26 27 28 10 9 8 7 6 5 4 3 2 1
001–341822–Mar/2024

All rights reserved.

Without limiting the rights under the copyright reserved above, no part of this publication may be reproduced, stored in or introduced into a retrieval system, or transmitted, in any form, or by any means (electronic, mechanical, photocopying, recording, or otherwise), without the prior written permission of the copyright owner.
Published in Great Britain by Dorling Kindersley Limited

A catalog record for this book
is available from the Library of Congress.
ISBN: 978-0-5938-4252-2

DK books are available at special discounts when purchased in bulk for sales promotions, premiums, fundraising, or educational use. For details, contact: DK Publishing Special Markets, 1745 Broadway, 20th Floor, New York, NY 10019
SpecialSales@dk.com

Printed and bound in China

The publisher would like to thank the following for their kind permission to reproduce their images:
a=above; c=center; b=below; l=left; r=right; t=top; b/g=background

Alamy Stock Photo: Auscape International Pty Ltd / Jean-Paul Ferrero 26-7, Biosphoto / Fabrice Simon 13tr; **Dreamstime.com:** Monkeygreen 21tr, 30cl, Andrei Stepanov 8-9, Vampy1 19cb; **naturepl.com:** Norbert Wu 23c; **PunchStock:** Digital Vision / Tim Hibo 6-7b; **Shutterstock.com:** Sergey 402 4-5b, Wirestock Creators 18-19

Cover images: *Front:* **Dreamstime.com:** Anastasiya Aheyeva cra, Vladimir Melnikov bl

All other images © Dorling Kindersley
For more information see: www.dkimages.com

www.dk.com

MIX
Paper | Supporting
responsible forestry
FSC™ C018179

This book was made with Forest Stewardship Council™ certified paper - one small step in DK's commitment to a sustainable future.
**For more information go to
www.dk.com/our-green-pledge**

Level
1

FROZEN
Worlds

Caryn Jenner

Contents

The Arctic

The Arctic is a very cold place.

Brrr!
It is at the top
of Earth.

The Arctic Ocean
is full of ice.

Arctic

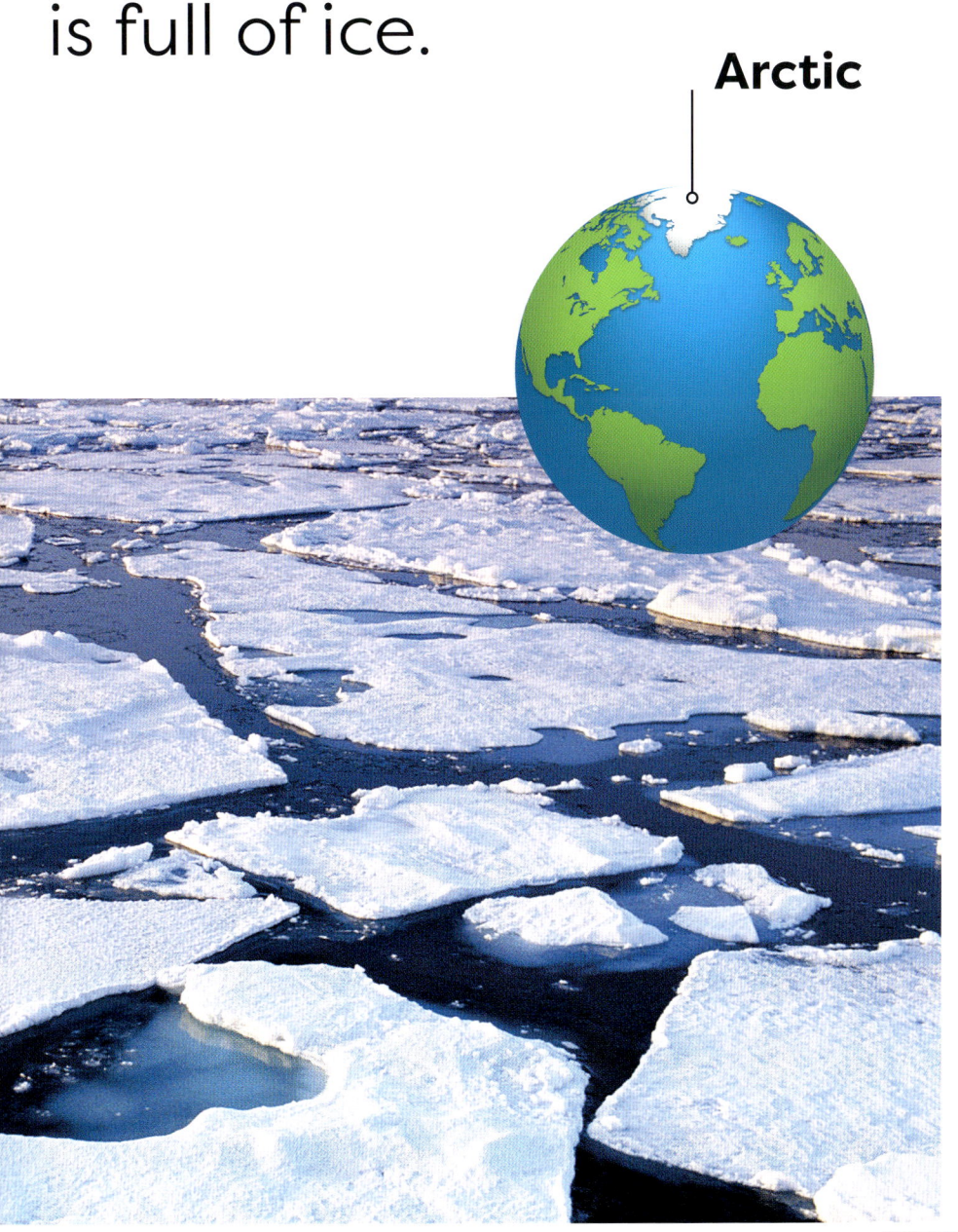

Plants in the Arctic

The land in the Arctic
is rocky.
The ground is frozen.
Many plants
still grow here.

People in the Arctic

These children
live in the Arctic.
They dress warmly
to play in the snow.

Polar Bears

Polar bears live
in the Arctic, too.
These furry animals
like to eat fish.

caribou

On the Move

A caribou pulls a sleigh across the snow.

sleigh

Zoom!
Here comes
a snowmobile.

snowmobile

Antarctica

Antarctica is at
the bottom of Earth.

It is even colder than the Arctic!

Antarctica

Land in Antarctica

Antarctica has many mountains.
The mountains are covered with snow and ice.

The rest of Antarctica is, too!

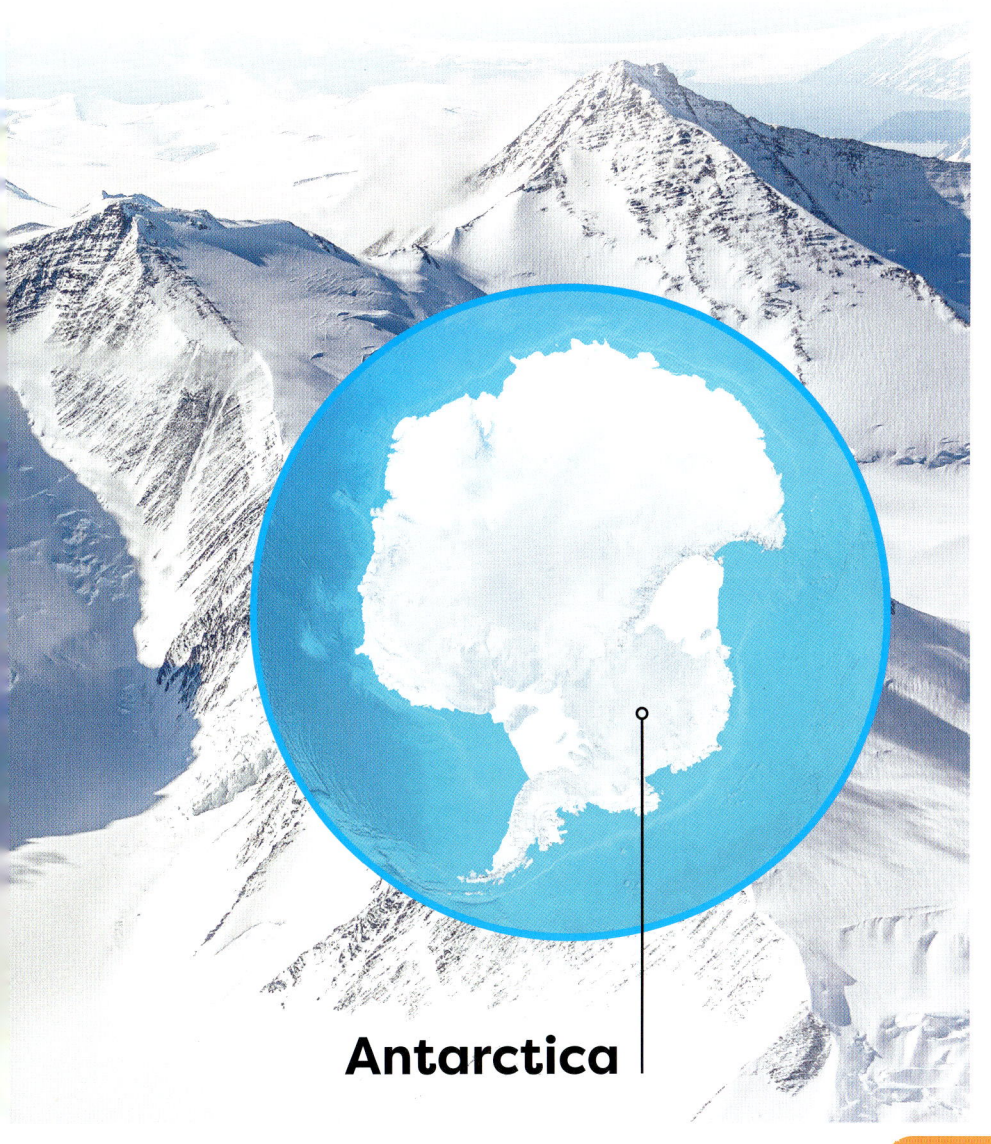

Antarctica

Icebergs

Big icebergs float
in the sea.
The icebergs melt.

Drip, drip.

iceberg

Penguins

Emperor penguins
live in Antarctica.

They swim in the cold sea and look for fish to eat.

Sea Animals

Splash!
A whale leaps out
of the water.

A seal watches
from the rocks.

Seasons

The Arctic has
two seasons.
Antarctica does, too.

In summer, it is always sunny.
In winter, it is always dark.

Light Show

Sometimes, the night sky lights up in many colors.

What an amazing sight!

Glossary

Antarctica
a cold place at the bottom of Earth

Arctic
a cold place at the top of Earth

iceberg
a huge floating piece of ice in an ocean

sleigh
a wagon that is pulled by an animal over snow

snowmobile
a machine that travels over snow and ice

Index

Quiz

Answer the questions to see what you have learned. Check your answers with an adult.

1. Where is the Arctic?

2. True or False: No plants grow in the Arctic.

3. Where is Antarctica?

4. What are three animals that live in Antarctica?

5. How are the Arctic and Antarctica the same as where you live? How are they different?

1. At the top of Earth 2. False 3. At the bottom of Earth
4. Emperor penguins, whales, and seals 5. Answers will vary

Fast
Animals

DK | Penguin Random House

THIS EDITION
Editorial Management by Oriel Square
Produced for DK by WonderLab Group LLC
Jennifer Emmett, Erica Green, Kate Hale, *Founders*

Editors Grace Hill Smith, Libby Romero, Maya Myers, Michaela Weglinski;
Photography Editors Kelley Miller, Annette Kiesow, Nicole DiMella;
Managing Editor Rachel Houghton; **Designers** Project Design Company;
Researcher Michelle Harris; **Copy Editor** Lori Merritt; **Indexer** Connie Binder; **Proofreader** Larry Shea;
Reading Specialist Dr. Jennifer Albro; **Curriculum Specialist** Elaine Larson

Published in the United States by DK Publishing
1745 Broadway, 20th Floor, New York, NY 10019

Copyright © 2023 Dorling Kindersley Limited
DK, a Division of Penguin Random House LLC
24 25 26 27 28 10 9 8 7 6 5 4 3 2 1
001–341623–Mar/2024

All rights reserved.

Without limiting the rights under the copyright reserved above, no part of this publication may be reproduced, stored in or introduced into a retrieval system, or transmitted, in any form, or by any means (electronic, mechanical, photocopying, recording, or otherwise), without the prior written permission of the copyright owner.
Published in Great Britain by Dorling Kindersley Limited

A catalog record for this book
is available from the Library of Congress.
ISBN: 978-0-5938-4166-2

DK books are available at special discounts when purchased in bulk for sales promotions, premiums, fundraising, or educational use. For details, contact: DK Publishing Special Markets, 1745 Broadway, 20th Floor, New York, NY 10019
SpecialSales@dk.com

Printed and bound in China

The publisher would like to thank the following for their kind permission to reproduce their images:
a=above; c=center; b=below; l=left; r=right; t=top; b/g=background

123RF.com: Eric Isselee / isselee 19bl, smileus 25bl; **Alamy Stock Photo:** Rick & Nora Bowers 27bl, Dominique Braud / Dembinsky Photo Associates 6-7, Michael Patrick O'Neill 5br, Kevin Schafer 11br; **BluePlanetArchive.com:** Michael Patrick O'Neill 10-11; **Dreamstime.com:** Adwo 1b, John Anderson 31clb, Rinus Baak 18br, 31cl, Natalia Bachkova 31cla, Bryan Busovicki 29bl, Harry Collins 23cr, Donyanedomam 8-9, 9bl, Ecophoto 16bc, Natalia Golovina 16-17, Ken Griffiths 22-23, 23bl, Japonikus 14br, 15b, Roger Johansen 5tr, Cathy Keifer / Cathykeifer 18-19, Matthijs Kuijpers 12cb, Mikael Males 7br, 31bl, Jan Pokorn / Pokec 25br, Stu Porter 4-5, 28br, 29tr, 29br, Slowmotiongli 17bl, John Stocker 6cb; **Getty Images:** imageBROKER / Jurgen & Christine Sohns 24-25, The Image Bank / Winfried Wisniewski 3cb, 30; **Getty Images / iStock:** E+ / Freder 28-29, Thierry Eidenweil 20-21, Edward Palm 14-15, the4js 26br; **naturepl.com:** Karine Aigner 26-27, Juergen Freund 11bl; **Shutterstock.com:** Gerald Robert Fischer 21bc, NickEvansKZN 13br, Cormac Price 12-13, Ferdy Timmerman 31tl, Brian A Wolf 7bl

Cover images: *Front:* **Dreamstime.com:** Martin Malchev, Anastasia Maslova cl; **Getty Images / iStock:** Godruma b; *Back:* **Dreamstime.com:** Yayamayka cra

All other images © Dorling Kindersley
For more information see: www.dkimages.com

www.dk.com

This book was made with Forest Stewardship Council™ certified paper - one small step in DK's commitment to a sustainable future.
For more information go to www.dk.com/our-green-pledge

Pre-level

Fast
Animals

Ruth A. Musgrave

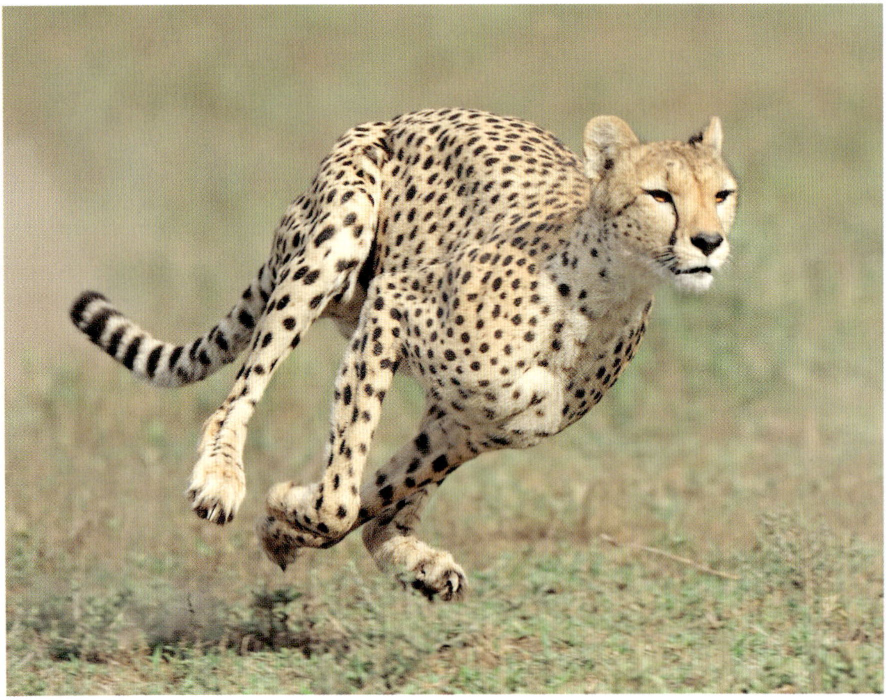

Animals run, fly, and swim.
Let's race to find fast animals.

This baby runs fast.
It runs faster than
a child.

pronghorn antelope

This bird flaps its wings fast.
Can you see its wings?

broad-tailed hummingbird

This turtle swims fast.
Big fish want
to eat it.
It swims fast
to get away.

**leatherback
sea turtle**

Other animals want
to eat this snake.
It moves fast
to get away.
It moves as fast as
a person riding a bike.

black mamba

dragonfly

This bug flies fast
to catch its food.
It grabs other bugs
from the air.

This bird
cannot fly.
It runs fast.
It takes
big steps.
One step is
as long
as a car.

ostrich

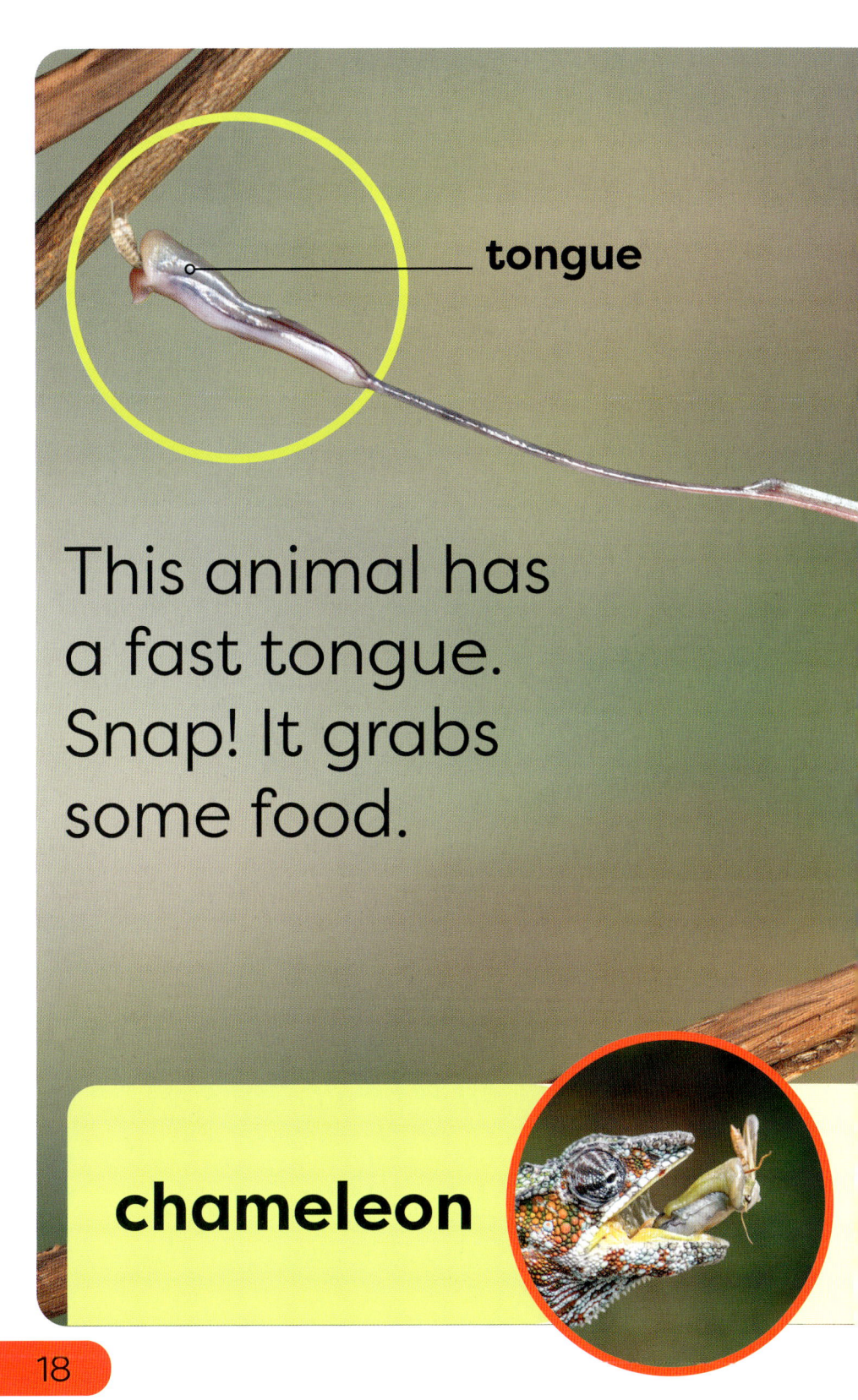

tongue

This animal has
a fast tongue.
Snap! It grabs
some food.

chameleon

This shrimp has
fast claws.
It uses them
to catch food.

**peacock
mantis shrimp**

This bird dives fast.
It is the fastest diver.
It catches other birds
in the air.

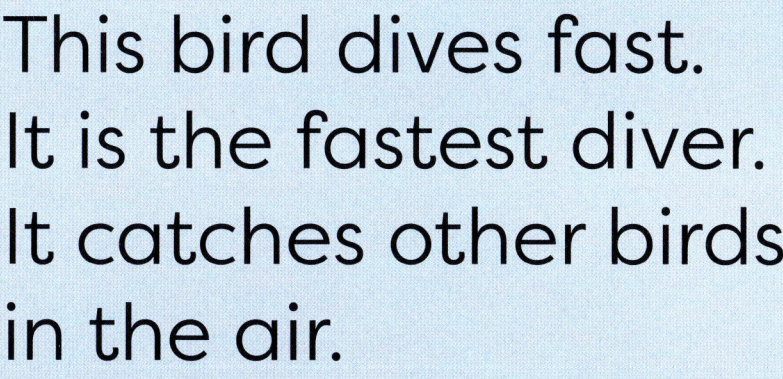

peregrine falcon

Hop, hop.
This animal hops fast.
It has big feet
and strong legs.

kangaroo

This bat flies fast.
It races through
the air.
It catches bugs
to eat.

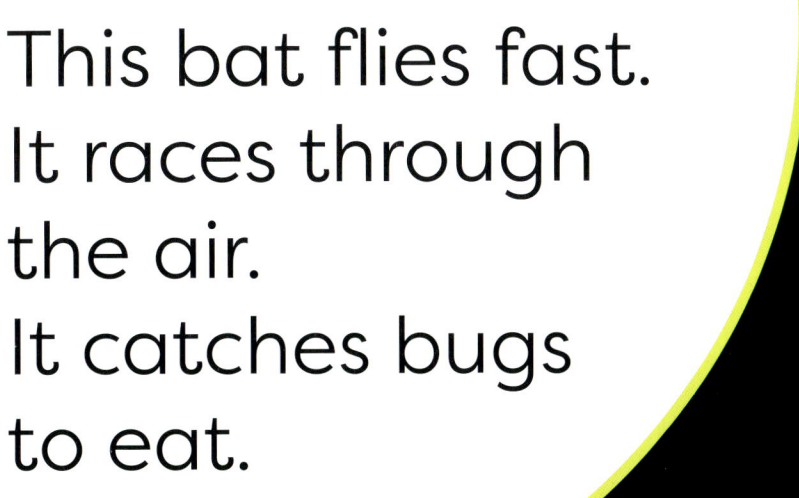

free-tailed bat

This cat runs fast.
It is the fastest runner
on land.
It races to catch
its food.

cheetah

Fast animals are everywhere.
They move fast to find food or to stay safe.
Which one would you like to be?

Glossary

chameleon
a reptile that lives in trees

dragonfly
an insect that lives near water and has four wings

hummingbird
a fast bird that drinks nectar from flowers

mantis shrimp
an ocean animal that hides in the sand

pronghorn antelope
an animal with hooves that lives in the grasslands

Quiz

Answer the questions to see what you've learned. Check your answers with an adult.

1. What kind of baby runs faster than you?

2. What bug catches other bugs from the air?

3. Which bird takes giant steps?

4. Which animal uses its claws to catch food?

5. What is the fastest cat in the world?

1. Pronghorn antelope 2. Dragonfly 3. Ostrich
4. Peacock mantis shrimp 5. Cheetah

Farm
Animals

FIRST EDITION
Series Editor Deborah Lock; **Designer** Sadie Thomas; **US Editor** Elizabeth Hester;
Pre-Production Producer Nadine King; **Producer** Sara Hu;
DTP Designer Almudena Díaz and Pilar Morales; **Jacket Designer** Simon Oon;
Reading Consultant Linda Gambrell, PhD

THIS EDITION
Editorial Management by Oriel Square
Produced for DK by WonderLab Group LLC
Jennifer Emmett, Erica Green, Kate Hale, *Founders*

Editors Grace Hill Smith, Libby Romero, Michaela Weglinski;
Photography Editors Kelley Miller, Annette Kiesow, Nicole DiMella;
Managing Editor Rachel Houghton; **Designers** Project Design Company;
Researcher Michelle Harris; **Copy Editor** Lori Merritt; **Indexer** Connie Binder; **Proofreader** Larry Shea;
Reading Specialist Dr. Jennifer Albro; **Curriculum Specialist** Elaine Larson

Published in the United States by DK Publishing
1745 Broadway, 20th Floor, New York, NY 10019

Copyright © 2024 Dorling Kindersley Limited
DK, a Division of Penguin Random House LLC
24 25 26 27 28 10 9 8 7 6 5 4 3 2 1
001–341623–Mar/2024

All rights reserved.
Without limiting the rights under the copyright reserved
above, no part of this publication may be reproduced, stored
in or introduced into a retrieval system, or transmitted, in any
form, or by any means (electronic, mechanical, photocopying,
recording, or otherwise), without the prior written permission
of the copyright owner.
Published in Great Britain by Dorling Kindersley Limited

A catalog record for this book
is available from the Library of Congress.
ISBN: 978-0-5938-4166-2

DK books are available at special discounts when purchased
in bulk for sales promotions, premiums, fundraising, or
educational use. For details, contact: DK Publishing Special Markets,
1745 Broadway, 20th Floor, New York, NY 10019
SpecialSales@dk.com

Printed and bound in China

The publisher would like to thank the following for their kind permission to reproduce their images:
a=above; c=center; b=below; l=left; r=right; t=top; b/g=background

123RF.com: Olga Itina 24-25; **Agefotostock.com:** imagebroker 14-15; **Dreamstime.com:** Melanie Hobson 12cl;
Shutterstock.com: Bigandt.com 15t

Cover images: *Front:* **Dreamstime.com:** Kateryna Firsova b; **Shutterstock.com:** Merggy, Pogorelova Olga crb;
Back: **Dreamstime.com:** Ernest Akayeu cla

All other images © Dorling Kindersley

www.dk.com

This book was made with Forest
Stewardship Council™ certified
paper - one small step in DK's
commitment to a sustainable future.
**For more information go to
www.dk.com/our-green-pledge**

Pre-level

Farm
Animals

Come and meet
my friends
on the farm.

farmhouse

barn

feathers

chickens

Here is the chicken
with her little chicks.

chick

Here is the turkey
coming to meet you.

snood

turkeys

feathers

Here is the pig.
Here are three
pink piglets.

piglet

pigs

ear

Here are the cows looking at you.

udder

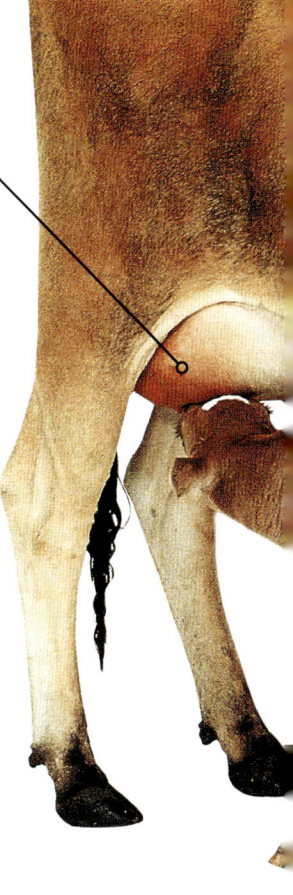

cows

calf

hoof

Here is the dog.
Here are her
sleepy puppies.

puppy

nose

dogs

Here is the sheep with two little lambs.

lamb

sheep

wool

ear

nose

goats

Here is the goat
lying down
with her kid.

kid

Here are the ducks with their fluffy ducklings.

beak

 **ducks**

duckling

Here are the white geese looking around.

geese

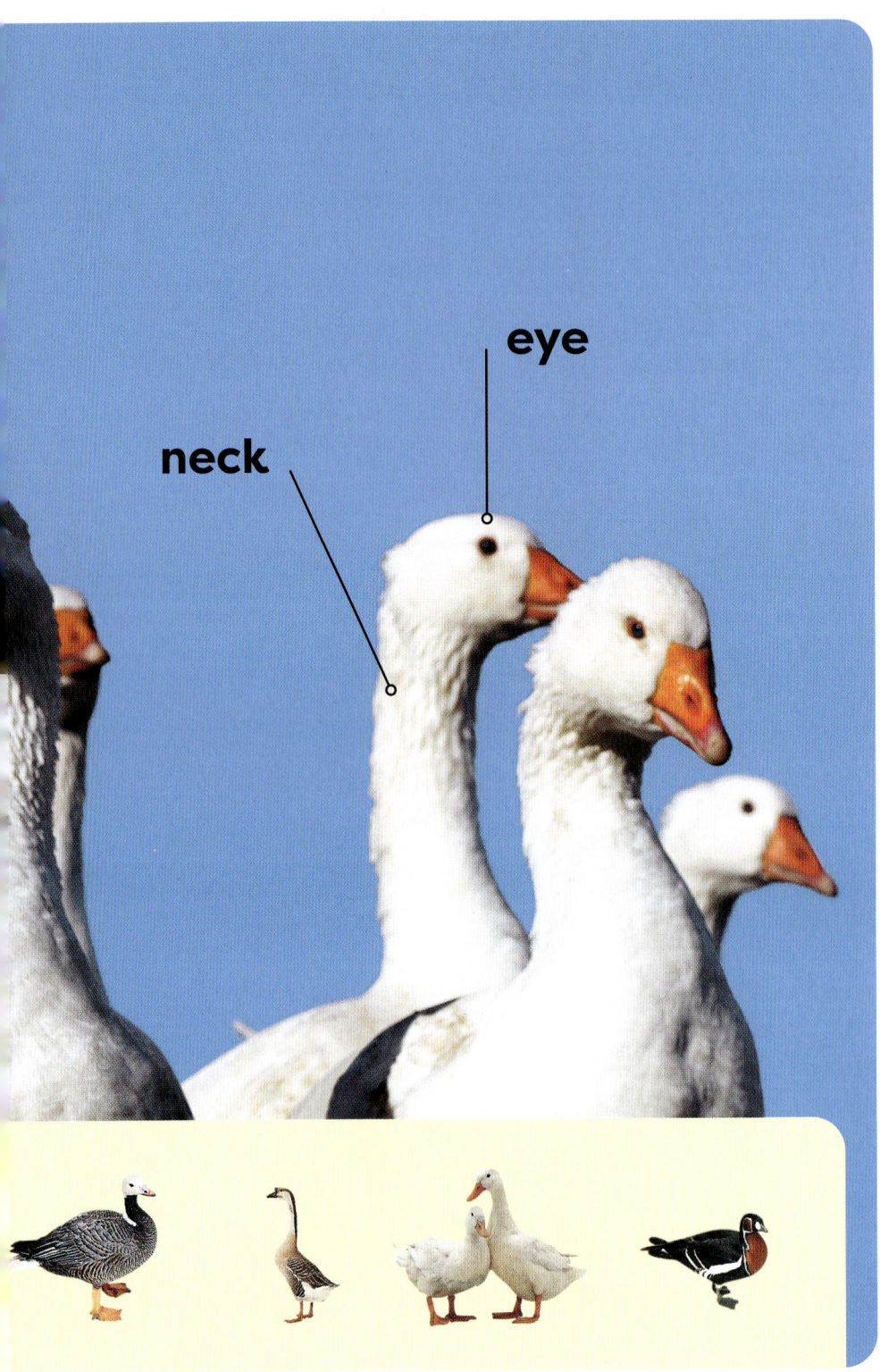

eye

neck

Here is the horse running with her foal.

horses

mane

foal

Here are two little ponies.

pony

ponies

Here is the cat curled up with her kitten.

kitten

cats

ear

Come see us again soon!

Glossary

chicken
a bird that is raised by people for its eggs

cow
a large, hoofed animal that is kept for its milk

dog
a four-legged animal that can herd sheep and cows

horse
a hoofed animal used for riding and farm work

sheep
an animal with a thick coat that is raised for wool

Quiz

Answer the questions to see what you have learned. Check your answers with an adult.

Which animal am I?

1. I am a baby chicken.
2. I am a pink animal with a round snout and big ears.
3. I am a baby cow.
4. I am a baby sheep.
5. I am a bird that likes to swim.

1. A chick 2. A pig (or piglet) 3. A calf 4. A lamb 5. A duck